Sissinghurst
Castle Garden

Adam Nicolson

🌳 **National Trust**

Opposite *the view
towards the
White Garden*

Introduction

Opposite *Harold and Vita in her writing room in the Tower at Sissinghurst*

Past and present

Sissinghurst is more than a garden. It is a garden in the ruin of a great Elizabethan house, set in the middle of its own woods, streams and farmland and with long views across the fields and meadows of the Kentish landscape. When Harold Nicolson, the writer and diplomat, and Vita Sackville-West, poet, novelist and gardener, first came here in 1930, they did not think they were making something new. Sissinghurst for them was no exercise in the modern or the pioneering. It was part of 'our romantic Saxon, Roman, Tudor Kent', as he described it. The wringing wet ruins they found were an opportunity to make a garden which drew on that sense of an abandoned past. Sissinghurst was dripping in its own inheritance:

Hushed and drowsy

Again and again, whenever Vita wrote about Sissinghurst, the atmosphere she summoned was of that embedded history, a certain rich slowness, even a druggedness, as if evening, when colours are soft and thickened, were its natural and fullest condition:

The heavy golden sunshine enriched the old brick with a kind of patina, and made the tower cast a long shadow across the grass, like the finger of a gigantic sundial veering slowly with the sun. Everything was hushed and drowsy and silent, but for the coo of the white pigeons sitting alone together on the roof.... They climbed the seventy-six steps of her tower and stood on the leaden flat, leaning their elbows on the parapet, and looking out in silence over the fields, the woods, the hop gardens, and the lake down in the hollow from which a faint mist was rising.

it had been a medieval manor house, its moat, in Vita's words, 'a black mirror of quiet water', then a 16th-century prodigy house, visited by both Mary and Elizabeth, England's great Renaissance queens, before falling into ruins and being mistreated over nearly 300 years. Harold and Vita knew that they had a chance here to revitalise a once-great but deeply neglected place, to take a ruin and make it flower.

Classical and romantic

Sissinghurst became, inevitably, a reflection of its makers. Much has been made of the marriage of sensibilities which the garden represents: a certain classical elegance and even austerity in the planning by Harold; a rich and romantic profusion in the planting, mostly by Vita; and a mutuality in these qualities, each becoming more itself through the presence of the other. Would the long crossing vistas of the garden, or the extraordinary strictness of the Yew Walk, seem quite so authoritative and so inevitable, if not surrounded by the fullness and lushness of the gardens they connect and separate? And would that fullness, what Vita called the 'cram, cram, cram, every chink and cranny' method, seem quite as beautiful if not contained and controlled by the decorum and order in which they were framed?

All of that is true, even if not in quite so schematic a way. Often it was Vita who advocated a simplicity in design; often it was Harold who wanted a more baroque and theatrical effect. Besides, this interfolding of aesthetic qualities was by 1930 commonplace. As William Robinson, the late Victorian gardening guru, had written years before, 'Formality is often essential to the plan of a garden but never to the arrangement of its flowers and shrubs.' Nevertheless, at Sissinghurst this double principle achieves a remarkably complete resolution.

Public and private

Sissinghurst was always, strangely, both a private and a public place. They first opened the garden to the public for two days in 1937, the entrance fee sixpence in an old tobacco tin, if you noticed it, on an old card table in the entrance arch. Vita would happily meet and chat to the visitors who accosted her. Harold could be ruder: 'A dreadful woman bursts in upon us,' he wrote in his diary of an unexpected photographer from *Picture Post*. 'I am very firm. But Vita with her warm-heartedness is weak. She calls it "being polite." Anyhow I refuse to be photographed, and go off and weed. I am weeding away, grunting under a forsythia, when I realise she is behind me with her camera. All she can have photographed was a large grey-flannel bottom.'

Vita's long series of articles in the *Observer* from 1947 until 1961 subtly and even surreptitiously, without actually naming Sissinghurst, advertised the garden to the wider world. It was something she longed to put on show. Vita was enthusiastic when the BBC wanted to make a Sissinghurst documentary in the mid-1950s. Harold was not keen on 'exposing my intimate affections to the public gaze'. But when both of them were first conceiving of the White Garden – and it is scarcely ever remembered that the planting was as much Harold's as Vita's idea – it was with a view to what it would look like to the public. 'I believe that when we scrap the delphiniums,' he wrote to her on 5 July 1949, 'we shall find the grey and white garden very beautiful... I want the garden as a whole to be superb in 1951 for the British Fair or Festival, with heaps of overseas visitors, and many will come down by car.'

Sissinghurst was, at one level, always a show, and yet something else persists beyond the display. For all its fame and publicity, the garden is still capable of touching many thousands of people as a profoundly private place, somewhere that seems consciously removed from the world. This garden from the beginning has always been an oasis of beauty in a world that is often indifferent to it.

And one of the reasons Sissinghurst can continue to play that role is that it seems to enshrine a set of ever deeper privacies, gathering inwards in concentric rings: first, the world of the farm and its woods, down and away from the road; then, the way in through the entrance arch into the garden itself; then, the private enclosures of each of the smaller gardens contained within the garden; then, the Tower, the great fixed point at the centre of it all, visible from every part; and finally, in imagination anyway, into Vita's writing room within the Tower, a scarcely visited place in her lifetime, the heart of Sissinghurst and its nest of privacies.

It was here in 1931, in her room on the first floor, that Vita wrote the poem which she called simply *Sissinghurst*. It was the best thing, Harold thought, she ever wrote, and she dedicated it to Virginia Woolf, who had been her lover. Far more than Vita's garden-writing ever could, the poem addresses the core of Sissinghurst. It is a place apart:

> Buried in time and sleep,
> So drowsy, overgrown,
> That here the moss is green upon the stone,
> And lichen stains the keep.

Time has almost stopped. A kind of enriched stagnancy colours the place and her vision of it. Sissinghurst, like the depths of its darkened moat, becomes a pool in which Vita can feel both ecstatically alive and at the same time suspended from the real world:

> For here, where days and years have lost
> their number,
> I let a plummet down in lieu of date,
> And lose myself within a slumber,
> Submerged, elate.

Those last two words are the essence of Vita's Sissinghurst, a freedom found in a deep absorption with place, land and the sense of a treasured past, a past that was better than the present, drenched into these bricks and this soil.

In *Orlando*, Virginia Woolf's fictional biography of Vita as a dazzling, multiple creature moving effortlessly through genders and times, she described the young and beautiful Elizabethan gazing from an oak-crowned knoll at the Kentish landscape, its leafy riches and summer brilliance:

> Nineteen English counties could be seen beneath, and on clear days thirty, or forty perhaps, if the weather was very fine. Sometimes one could see the English Channel, wave reiterating upon wave. Rivers could be seen and pleasure boats gliding on them; and galleons setting out to sea; and armadas with puffs of smoke from which came the dull thud of cannon firing; and forts on the coast; and castles among the meadows…

But that beauty and vibrancy was not enough. The young Vita-Orlando needed something more. Having drunk on what he had seen, the young man 'flung himself on the earth at the foot of the oak tree. He loved, beneath all this summer transiency, to feel the earth's spine beneath him; for he felt the need of something which he could attach his floating heart to.' Those words are the most evocative description ever made of what Sissinghurst came to mean to Vita. This was the place where, in the end, she could tether her floating heart.

Tour of the Garden

The view from the Tower

Any visitor to Sissinghurst should begin by climbing the Elizabethan Tower and surveying the garden and the wider estate from its rooftop platform. Almost certainly, that is what the Tower, which was probably built in the 1560s, was meant for. The buildings at Sissinghurst, and this tower as their central point, were almost exactly in the middle of the 700-acre, near-circular deer park. A park pale, to keep the deer in and poachers out, was built around the perimeter. Remains of the bank on which it was set have been discovered in the surrounding woods and fields. Intriguingly, for about three-quarters of its length, in every direction except the north-east, that park pale was on the skyline seen from the top of the Tower. The park pale, the deer park itself and the Elizabethan tower were, in other words, all part of a single, integrated aesthetic experience: the rim, body and hub of a giant hunting ground, all of it visible from the most convenient and elegant of viewing platforms. It is quite conceivable that Queen Elizabeth I, on her visit here in August 1573, climbed these turret steps and viewed the surrounding country exactly as we do today.

Later landscape changes – the insertion of hedges, the growth of the wood – have largely obliterated the Sissinghurst park, but nearer to hand one can get an instant feeling for the sight that faced Harold and Vita on their first arrival in 1930. Remove from your mind's eye all sense of colour and precision. There are no stripy lawns. The place is abandoned. Mounds of rubbish lie in the gaps between the ancient walls and the two cottages now embedded in the garden. There is no Yew Walk. To the south, there are vegetables growing in what is now the Rose Garden. The long front range consists of cottages to the south, a filthy stable block to the north. Vita, gazing at the pink bricks, told her thirteen-year-old son Nigel that 'we shall be very happy here'. He was horrified. All he saw was 'the mess, the unattractiveness, the uninhabitability of the place'.

What is now the entrance archway was blocked and filled with farm labourers' living quarters. 'Old bedsteads, old plough-shares, old cabbage stalks, old broken down earth closets, old matted wire and mountains of sardine tins, all muddled up in a tangle of bindweed, nettles and ground elder': that was the state to which Sissinghurst had sunk, 'a castle running away into sordidness and squalor, a garden crying out for rescue'. Only in the corner of the orchard did they find an ancient rose, known as *R. Gallica* 'Sissinghurst Castle', flowering, they hoped, where the Elizabethan gardeners had planted it.

On to this intractable set of circumstances Harold Nicolson imposed his firm but delicate sense of order. It was far from easy, and in 1953 Vita wrote in sympathy for his task:

> The walls were not all at right angles to one another; the courtyard was not rectangular but coffin-shaped; the Tower was not opposite the main entrance… All this was disconcerting, and there were also minor crookednesses which had somehow to be camouflaged. I do not think you would notice them from ground-level now; though if you ascended the tower and looked down, you might still give a sympathetic thought to the worried designer, with his immense sheets of ruled paper and his measuring tapes and his India rubbers, pushing his fingers through his rumpled hair, trying to get the puzzle worked out.

There were times, she said, when 'after weeks of paper struggle he would come home to discover that

I had stuck some tree or shrub bang in the middle of his projected path or gateway.'

Despite this – and both teased the other about the hopelessness of their aesthetic prejudices – they had agreed on the principles from the start. Two long axes – one running from the entrance arch through the Tower and down to the statue of Dionysus beyond the moat; another at right angles to it, from the Spring Garden through the Rose Garden, the lower courtyard and into the White Garden – would cross on the lawn just below the Tower. Other axes were made to echo these two main vistas, and opening off

them a set of relatively small, simply laid out gardens would provide the destinations which these lines of promise led one to expect. In plan, Sissinghurst is a conversation between invitation and delight, a constant suggestion of what might be beyond the next hedge or wall, but no revelation of what that was until you reached it.

The experience of walking around the garden is in that way a sequence of arrivals. It can surprise but it never shocks, nor intends to. The garden's purpose, perhaps, is calm. It has the effortlessness and efficiency of a well-made piece of furniture.

The Top Courtyard

Dominated by the Tower (which causes severe downdraughts in a wind and means the gardeners have to be careful about tying up the roses, vines and clematis, if they are not to collapse in a gale), the Top Courtyard is the first course of Sissinghurst's banquet. As a beginning, it is careful and quiet. You have come in through the entranceway arch, passing the four 19th-century bronze urns which Vita's mother had inherited from the Wallace Collection in Paris, and you find yourself in a cool green space walled on all sides. The lawn, or at least the subtle interplay of pink and green which the lawn and buildings create, establishes the quiet and unassertive atmosphere, something of which Harold was quite conscious. 'Our superb climate conditions our style – the English lawn is the basis of our garden design,' he wrote. 'The garden designer must recognize that the foundations of any good English garden are water, trees, hedges and lawn.'

Mowing the grass

Particularly on the edges of paths and at narrow entrances, the lawns take enormous amounts of wear. To keep the grass (a ryegrass-based mix called Olympic Sportsground) growing strongly throughout the season, a slow-release fertiliser is spread on them in February. Areas of heavy wear get a pick-up of a seaweed-based liquid feed later in the year. Every lawn is then mown once a week, taking ten hours for the whole garden, the mowers set at ⅞ of an inch, with each stripe always mown in the same direction to keep the pattern crisp. The top lawn is mown on the diagonal, to conceal the fact that the courtyard is far from rectangular, and in double width, 48-inch stripes to make a stronger, bolder impact which matches the scale of the courtyard.

The sense of orderliness now is different from how Sissinghurst was in 1930: there were no stone paths; ramshackle buildings of various dates were tacked on the Tudor original. A 19th-century painting shows sheep and cows happily grazing here. The courtyard was open to the north, and for a while Vita and Harold thought of moving the Elizabethan barn to fill the gap. Harold had other more or less elaborate ideas – busts of modern 'Worthies' was one, a loggia or 'cave' in the north wall another – but in the end simplicity triumphed. A tall, simple wall, on ancient foundations which had survived, was built to back the courtyard's high point: the south-facing Purple Border.

The Purple Border

Gertrude Jekyll, the grandmother of Sissinghurst's gardening style, had always warned against massed purples for their tendency to heaviness. Vita's plunging into the forbidden territory may have been an act of conscious rebellion. In fact the Purple Border is not just made up of purples; it is a mix of pink, blues, lilacs and purples.

Extreme care goes into producing a relaxed effect: purple-leaved plants are lightened by silver cardoons and tall salvias. Hazel brushwood, buried within the foliage, supports most of the plants. Flowers are deadheaded every Friday as they go over. Every winter, plants are moved and replaced. And in recent years, the border's highpoint in late summer has been extended at both ends of the season, with tulips, wallflowers, irises and dahlias.

Other beds in this courtyard are deliberately planted so as not to rival this show-stopper, but at eye-level a series of stone sinks set against the long front range are filled with exquisite species tulips, hyacinths, auriculas and other delicacies, changed throughout the year.

Opposite The Top Courtyard, 'the first course of Sissinghurst's banquet' **Above** *The Purple Border is a complex tapestry of purples ranging from violet-blue through to crimson-magenta and every shade in between. Spring brings with it a first wave of colour, with tulips, wallflowers and* Lunaria annua

The Library

At the north end of the front range, Vita and Harold made their library-cum-sitting room, which they called the Big Room. Since Elizabethan times, it had been the stables, the hunters and cart-horses walking in and out through the wide door opening. The way Vita and Harold remade the room is full of echoes of Knole, the great Sackville house near Sevenoaks in which Vita had grown up: the high desk and the wigstands, the silver sconces, and the paintings of Vita's Sackville ancestors – poets, statesmen, rakes – all contribute to a sense that this room is a remaking of that other house which, if she had been a boy, she would have inherited.

'They are there still,' Vita wrote about Knole, 'chairs, stools, sofas, love-seats, their original

coverings untouched by man but softened by time. They stand beneath the portraits of the men and women who sat in them; the great four-poster beds still stand in the rooms of the men and women who slept in them, drawing the curtains closely around them.' In a sense, the Big Room at Sissinghurst can be seen as Vita's record of her disinheritance, a break in the continuity she loved.

The portrait of Vita over the fireplace by Philip de László shows her in 1909, when she was a few days short of her 17th birthday. 'Do you not think,' the unfortunate painter was asked by Vita's mother, the fearsomely eccentric Lady Sackville, who had commissioned the portrait, 'that you owe it to your art and to her beauty to paint her without a fee?' Vita hated the picture for what she saw as its Edwardian vacuity, and during her lifetime it remained in the attic.

The Rose Garden

At the southern end of the Top Courtyard, a small gateway leads into the Rose Garden. At its highpoint in late June and early July, it exudes a sumptuous richness which re-enacts year after year precisely the 'tumble of roses and honeysuckle, figs and vines' which Vita had envisaged. Harold's strict geometry is centred on the circular hedged space of the Rondel (the name given to oasthouse floors) and, at the west end, the apse-like curve of the wall they built in 1934. Between them is unbroken voluptuousness, an enveloping surprise after the clarity of the Top Courtyard. Irises, alliums, peonies, Japanese anemones and eremurus are planted in among the mounded roses, 'foaming in the midst of the flower borders'. Figs, vines, more roses and clematises are trained on the walls. There is little bare soil to be seen, and the garden is as thick with scent and colour as any eastern bazaar. As Anne Scott-James described it, this was exactly the point:

> The romance of the old roses appealed to Vita as much as their beauty and scent. She liked the roses which looked like flowers from a tapestry, the roses with a long history, like the dark red Gallic rose probably brought from Persia by the Arabs in the seventh century, and the roses with evocative names, like Cardinal de Richelieu or Comtesse du Cayla, who was the mistress of Louis XVIII …

This part of Sissinghurst was used as a kitchen garden until 1937, but in that year the roses which were overflowing the space that would later become the White Garden were transferred here. Roses could summon from Vita the richest of her garden writing. Here, as she wrote, she liked to remember:

> those dusky mysterious hours in an Oriental storehouse where the rugs and carpets of Isfahan and Bokhara and Samarcand were unrolled in their dim but sumptuous colouring and richness of texture for slow delight. Rich they were, rich as a fig broken, soft as a ripened peach, freckled as an apricot, coral as pomegranate, bloomy as a bunch of grapes. It is of these that the old roses remind me…

Left, top to bottom
Rosa moyesii, Rosa Mundi,
R. *'Constance Spry'*, R.
californica *'Plena'*.
Centre *The Rose Garden at
its height in June.* **Above, top
to bottom** R. *'Sissinghurst
Castle'*, R. *'Complicata'*, R.
'Nevada'

'I know also that most of them suffer from the serious drawback of flowering only once during a season, but what incomparable lavishness they give, while they are about it. There is nothing scrimpy or stingy about them. They have a generosity which is as desirable in plants as in people.' **Vita Sackville-West, writing about old roses**

Pruning the roses

In November, after the hedges have been cut, the gardeners turn to pruning the roses. They start with the climbers and ramblers – about 50 of them in the garden as a whole – first of all 'snibbling' them, a word that is apparently unique to Sissinghurst. It means cutting back all of the flowered side shoots to two to three buds, leaving a framework that can then be assessed. The next step is to remove at least some of the old woody stems either from the base or back to a really strong side shoot, in order to promote new growth. As pruning progresses the whole rose is carefully untied. Finally, the remaining stems are bent over into arcs that cover the wall and retied in their new positions. This not only looks very attractive but also breaks apical dominance so that flowers are produced all the way along each stem. In summer the walls are smothered with roses.

The non-climbing roses are trained either as spiralling stems up three or four stout chestnut poles or onto hazel 'benders'; poles that have been gently bent into arcs and pushed into the ground to form hoops. The strong rose stems are then tied on to the hazel or to each other to form a dome, each one a unique structure that creates interest in the beds and brings the roses down to eye level.

This way of training roses has been maintained here since before the war, brought from Cliveden by Jack Vass, who came to be Vita's head gardener at Sissinghurst in 1939. The roses are given a generous amount of well-rotted compost in the spring, as well as a dressing of potash and magnesium sulphate, and need to be sprayed about four times a year against blackspot and mildew. In the summer, a team of volunteers deadhead the roses in the Rose Garden every week, transforming it back to that magical moment when the Rose Garden glows with perfection.

'All the gardeners love rose-pruning,' as one of them, Helen Champion, says, 'because it is an absorbing combination of technical precision and creativity. There's a feeling of great satisfaction when each rose is finally trained on to its new structure ready for the season ahead. Even in deep winter, the domes and spirals of the roses have a stark beauty that stands out against the pale sky. It's exciting to think that hidden within their seemingly lifeless and skeletal forms lies the promise of good things to come.'

The Spring Garden

The Spring Garden, or the Lime Walk as it is also known, is reached from the path leading south from the Rondel. It was the one part of the garden in which Harold Nicolson controlled the planting as well as the design. Particularly in the late 1940s and 1950s, after he had left Parliament, he attended with great care to the details of every section: the long beds on either side, the pots that give some punctuation to the garden, the avenue of pleached limes and the small, intense patches of spring flowers which surround their feet.

Although Vita once compared its strict rectilinearity to Platform 5 at Charing Cross, she loved Harold for this garden. She wrote to him on 7 March 1950, after he had left for the week in London, just as the spring bulbs were breaking into flower:

> It has turned into the heavenly day we anticipated. Oh how I wish you were here! I walked down the Spring Garden and all your little flowers bit and tore at my heart. I do love you so, Hadji. It is quite simple: I do love you so. Just that.

Once you realise that the Spring Garden meant this much to them, it becomes, in a way, the core of Sissinghurst. They had travelled together in the Mediterranean, in North Africa and in Persia, where many of these flowers decorate the hillsides. Above all they loved the wild tulips, the little scarlet one that was 'blood-red in the sun' and 'the white ones that are so sweet scented and the yellow ones that have no scent at all, but are of a beautiful pure buttercup yellow, like a pointed goblet designed by some early draughtsman with a right instinct for line'. That is the world the Spring Garden celebrates, not the simplicity of nature, but the exotic glamour of which nature, in these spring flowers, is capable.

Right The Lime Walk at the climax of spring, edged with cheerful Muscari armeniacum, Anemone apennina, Fritillaria meleagris, *daffodils, narcissi and tulips*

To get this effect of intense elegance required intense supervision and a readiness to ditch what didn't work. 'Il faut être impitoyable' ('One must be ruthless') was Harold's motto and although he had his own dedicated gardener here, Sidney Neve, Harold spent vast quantities of time making perfect what he called 'My Life's Work'. He recommended 'the trug and handfork system of weeding, which requires patience but no excessive industry, and by which one can without undue effort clear three square yards in as many hours.' It was a method that was 'good for soil and soul alike'.

He never thought he was that competent a gardener. 'Mummy is neat with garden work,' he once wrote to his son Nigel during the war, 'and from time to time she will glance up at my flounderings in affectionate contempt.'

The garden has changed slightly since his time. Its York stone slabs replace the extraordinary pink, yellow and green concrete paving he had originally installed. The limes have been replaced twice. In the 1950s, the beds were mixed flowery carpets, in which perennials and foxgloves interrupted the mats of spring bulbs. That was changed in the 1960s, to concentrate its impact into an unbroken six-week burst.

'The planting requires constant editing,' the Head Gardener Troy Smith says. 'Every year I assess the planting, taking snapshots of each bed every week. I can then decide which areas need tweaking or readjustment. I try to ensure there are flowers in a range of colours and shapes throughout all of the beds for the whole of the six-week period. If you are not careful the scillas and grape hyacinths, which are invasive, can take over.'

The system by which they maintain the brilliance is highly labour-intensive. Chosen bulbs are planted in four-inch pots in the autumn and then put into the ground in the spring when the leaves first appear. 'There is a lot of work in doing them like that,' Troy says, 'but it minimises disturbance of the existing bulbs and means we are not planting them out on to our heavy and cold clay soil. We like to put in special things like species fritillaries or Harold's Rembrandt tulips.'

The Cottage Garden

Just off the Spring Garden are the rich oranges, reds and yellows of the Cottage Garden. Don't be misled by the name. As the garden writer Tony Lord has said, 'This is as much a cottage garden as Marie-Antoinette was a milkmaid.' Four rather overlarge and matronly Irish yews dominate the centre of the garden, giving it a faintly wobbly and eccentric air. But they are surrounded by extreme gardening sophistication. Against the wall of the South Cottage, which is in fact a fragment of the Elizabethan house, the early-summer-flowering rose 'Mme Alfred Carrière' (known to Harold as 'Mrs Alfonso's Career') was the first thing they planted at Sissinghurst, on 6 May 1930, the very day their offer to buy was accepted.

The rest of the garden is filled with hot colours – a 'sunset' scheme which both Vita and Harold claimed as their idea – which reaches its peak in late summer and early autumn. But that climax is nowadays gradually approached throughout the spring and summer: tulips, wallflowers, aquilegias and arctotis – all in the warm, glowing colours which feed off the pink and burnt oranges of the Elizabethan brick – lead up to the moment when the full height of verbascum, red hot pokers (loathed by Harold), cannas, crocosmias and dahlias – as well as clumps of annuals including the beautiful deep crimson 'Velvet Queen' sunflower and 'Ladybird' corn poppies, with a deep black blodge on each petal – erupt into the most exotic of all Sissinghurst's gardens.

'Cram, cram, cram, every chink and cranny… I like generosity wherever I find it… Always exaggerate rather than stint. Masses are more effective than mingies.'

Vita Sackville-West

There is far more to it now than there ever was in Vita's day. It comes as some surprise to know that before the 1960s, there were no wallflowers in this garden, whereas their four or five varieties are now its mainstay in the spring. It is certainly gardened with an extravagantly bold and theatrical effect.

Harold's work room and Vita's bedroom and bathroom all looked on to the Cottage Garden. No garden here was more closely connected to their daily lives and it is full of what they would have called 'coffee-cups' – accidental reminders of a loved person: the coffee cup remaining on a table after a friend or lover had left.

Opposite, below and overleaf Famous for its hot colours, the Cottage Garden bursts into vibrant life in spring with wallflowers, tulips and mounds of euphorbias

On 27 October 1959 Vita wrote to Harold, about one of these, his 'scoop' – it is still there – a little hollow in one of the stones near the central copper basin. Harold used it each morning to measure how much rain had fallen in the night. He was in his London clothes, about to get the train to London for the week. 'I was thinking this morning how awful it would be if you died,' she wrote:

I do often think that; but it came over me all of a heap when I looked out of the bathroom window and saw you in your blue coat and black hat, peering into your scoop. It is the sort of sudden view of a person that twists one's heart, when they don't know you are observing them – they have an innocent look, almost as a child asleep – one feels one is spying on some secret life one should not know about. Anyway, the scoop would be the most poignant coffee-cup ever made.

I often think I have never told you how much I love you – and if you died I should reproach myself, saying: Why did I never tell him? Why did I never tell him enough?

'Cram, cram, cram'
'We want to have it jam-packed, as solid as we can get it. And get every shade if we can. We simply don't worry if this doesn't go with that. It is important that it doesn't end up all yellow. But it doesn't matter where things go, because they are all within that same orange, yellow and red range. And we are always looking how we can trickle little things through the beds, streaming colours and ideas from one bed to another.'
Wendy Tremenheere, Deputy Head Gardener

The Nuttery

In April 1930, Harold's diary recorded the moment he and Vita decided to buy the bleak broken ruin she had found. 'We come suddenly upon the nutwalk,' he wrote, 'and that settles it.' It was a plantation of Kentish cobnuts, a variety of hazel, probably then about 30 years old. Its presence here, like the one old rose in the orchard, was a sign, even under half a thicket of brambles, that cultivation was possible, that this could again become a beautiful place.

They called it correctly, but in a way that is reminiscent of the Arts and Crafts world of Gertrude Jekyll, the Nut Platt and underplanted the trees with a carpet of polyanthus. That too was a Jekyll idea, a brilliant brief springtime flowering always referred to by Harold as 'the company of the bright and good'. Invaded by celandines and chronically vulnerable to birds eating the buds, fungal attack and an ineradicable disease known simply as 'polyanthus sickness', by the mid-1960s it was fading and clearly had to go.

The scheme that replaced it, designed by Vita's last head gardeners Pam Schwerdt and Sibylle Kreutzberger, together with Graham Stuart Thomas, then the National Trust Gardens Adviser, remains, at its peak in late spring just as the Spring Garden fades, the most entrancingly beautiful sight at Sissinghurst.

Under the patchy shade of the cobnuts, drifts of green and yellow, splashed with blue and white, mimic a woodland floor, but one that has had magic blown across it. It bears the same relation to a real wood that the Spring Garden does to a real meadow: if most gardens coarsen natural beauty, these two heighten and refine it. Bright stands of the dark-loving *Euphorbia amygdaloides* var. *robbiae* glow in the shade of the nut trees. The fresh green of *Smyrnium perfoliatum* stands above rivers of orchids and white trilliums, white bluebells (any blue bluebell is removed as soon as it is seen) and wood anemones. Little oxslips (paler than cowslips, which are not allowed here – too yellow), *Omphalodes cappadocica* and delicate pink wood geraniums are scattered through the green and white.

Nothing has a stronger architectural presence here than the pleated leaves of *Veratrum nigrum*. Shuttlecock ferns unfold their fronds in the first weeks of summer, the bronze leaves of epimediums emerge, the extraordinary star geometry of *Paris polyphylla* (grown in the nursery here, often taking three or four years to germinate) appears among them, and by mid-July the performance is done, and the whole Nuttery is brown and over.

'We have extended the Nuttery,' Troy Smith, the Head Gardener, says, 'planting further to the south so that all of the Nut Platt is underplanted with the same magical mix of woodland plants, rather than a third of it put down to lawn. It is unclear as to how Harold and Vita treated this space and whether they too may have increased the polyanthus planting under the nuts to the south.'

'The flowers I like best are the flowers requiring a close inspection before they consent to reveal their innermost secret beauty.'

Vita Sackville-West

Opposite A restrained palette of green, white, lime-yellow and blue characterises the Nuttery, home to woodland plants chosen to thrive in shady conditions and blend in ever-changing, magical patterns of light and shade

'Climbers are among the most useful plants in any garden. They take up little ground space, and they can be employed for many purposes.'

Vita Sackville-West

The Moat Walk

Alongside the Nuttery, but strictly separated from it by a bank of golden yellow azaleas, is the Moat Walk. The elegant Elizabethan wall which defines the walk was only discovered under the rubbish and brambles when a gardener's pick struck it several weeks after Vita and Harold first arrived. Every year, the gardeners push perennial wallflowers into the nooks and crannies in the mortar, each bedded into their little compost plug. After the wall had been repointed in the 1970s, the gardeners simply attacked it with chisels, to recreate the holes the wallflowers needed. Where people stand to admire the white wisteria which flows over the top of the wall, what the gardeners call 'an admiration patch' of compacted soil and worn grass develops beneath it. It requires deep aeration with a special tool each autumn to rejuvenate the turf.

The azaleas – originally in many more various and violent colours than the gold of their rootstock to which they have now reverted – were planted in 1946 with the £100 Vita had won from the Royal Society of Literature's Heinemann Prize for her poem *The Garden*. It was the last poem she published, feeling

even as she was writing it an ebbing of the poetic gift and a dimming of the fire. The azaleas were disliked by Harold as 'suburban'; he preferred the bluebells beneath them, which had come up with the mulch of leaf mould from the wood. But Vita would not be put off her azaleas, and each May they burn as a memorial to her passion and her regret at its passing. She had no taste for the fading exhaustion of old age. 'My mood is like a fire that will not heat,' she wrote in *The Garden:*

> There's all the setting for a roar of flame
> But love and poetry are but a name
> And neither will my fuel burn nor I.
>
> Come flame; come, come tongue of courage;
>   scorch me, sear;
> I'll risk the burning to regain the clear
> Fangs of returning life as sharp as fire.
> Better, I swear, to be consumed entire
> Than smoulder, knowing neither zest nor fear.

'The Moat Walk underplanting now requires lifting and renewing,' Troy explains. 'We are looking at Vita's diaries and considering what to plant. I have in mind Vita and Harold's planting of polyanthus in the Nut Platt; this was such an iconic and special thing at Sissinghurst it would be lovely to get them back somewhere. We are also thinking about adding them on the top of the Moat Walk bank under the nuts and allowing them to run down the slope to the grass and across the path, and into the Nuttery.'

Opposite and above The Moat Walk is framed with climbing white wisteria on one side and golden yellow azaleas on the another, with the Tower standing sentinel in the distance. Wallflowers add colour and yet more scent to this late spring spectacle

The Herb Garden

Pushed right to the corner of the garden, where the oaks of the wood on the far side of the lake appear over its yew hedges, the Herb Garden was never conceived as an adjunct to a kitchen. It is a private place heady with the scent of the plants it contains.

The yew hedges were planted in 1934, but the garden was neglected during the war and became a field of ground elder. In 1946 it was started again with a crop of potatoes to clean the soil. The seat made of old fragments of the Elizabethan house and cushioned with camomile was the work of Jack Copper the handyman-chauffeur. The central marble bowl had been brought back from Constantinople where the Nicolsons lived when first married. Harold was a junior diplomat in the embassy, and it was there that Vita had cultivated her first garden.

This herb garden follows a traditional design: small beds so that herbs can be picked without any trampling. That of course remains a hazard in a garden open to the public. By the end of each summer, visible 'browse-horizons' from the visitors' gentle picking appear in the beds like the lines left on the trees by cattle in a park.

Since 2000, everything here, about 160 different sorts of herb, has been gardened organically, in the knowledge that visitors will sniff and taste the leaves. All but 35 of them are perennials, but some of them, such as hyssop, have to be replaced every four years

or so. It is a struggle to keep on top of the vigorous ones. Peter Fifield, who looks after this garden, likes to introduce new varieties: 'After all, Vita would have tried new plants. I like to go for plants which are known as herbs but which also have height and attractive flowers, such as marshmallow and cornflowers. Vita liked the literary connections and the folklore of herbs. I think it's fair to say that some of the plants are not necessarily elegant, pungent or beautiful, but just rather unusual.'

Between the Herb Garden and the moat is the thyme lawn, first planted in 1946 and a headache ever since. People used to walk on it, which killed the plants. Now it has been given a brick edge, which helps preserve it. But it is almost impossible to keep in the condition Sissinghurst expects and demands. Pam Schwerdt, one of the two head gardeners here between 1959 and 1990, thought it 'fun when it is really flowering and wobbling with bees, but it is not a labour-saving idea'.

All images *The Herb Garden follows a traditional design of small beds and narrow brick and stone paths. It is planted with a great number of herbs, including new varieties, following Vita's ethos of constant renewal and experimentation*

The Orchard

From the moment it was taken in hand in 1937, the Orchard was always intended to be half garden. Under the grass, there are still mounds of rubble, the footings of the long-demolished great house. Some of them emerge into islands of brick near the Yew Walk, but the rubble meant that most of the ground here could never be cultivated.

What was no good for gardening – many of the trees had given up producing fruit even by the 1930s – was perfect as a kind of wilderness, a place where the Sissinghurst aesthetic could relax. It was a transitional zone between garden and country, and in October 1937 Harold described to Vita his ideas for a path around the inner side of the moat 'edged with musk roses and irises and winding paths in the middle with dells, boskies, tangles – in fact, scope for everything but not garden flowers – wild roses, white foxgloves in droves, narcissus in regiments.'

By the 1950s and 1960s they had achieved something of this subtle middle ground, filling the trees with roses (musk, moss, rugosa and species). Vita loved above all the rose called 'Madame Plantier', three of which she trained up adjacent apple trees here. They poured 'down in a vast crinoline stitched all over it with white sweet-scented clusters of flowers… I go out to look at her in the moonlight,' she wrote. 'She gleams, a pear-shaped ghost, contriving to look both matronly and virginal. She has to be tied up round her tree, in long strands, otherwise she would make a big straggly bush.'

But it was also a place in which Vita and Harold's different ideals for the garden came into conflict. Vita's was deeply nostalgic and retrospective, a dream of what England had once been. One evening, in late August 1939, she went out in the Orchard to mow the hay:

> The scythe slid regularly through the long grass, laying the swathe quite neatly for so inexpert a mower, like fesses across a heraldic field… Not only did ripe apples drop about my head with big thuds into grass, falling from sheer maturity although not the frailest breeze arrived to stir the moonlight – but the scythe occasionally sliced through one of them with a juicy sound.

For Harold, though, there was a desire to formalise this Edenic looseness. 'You will recall how with tape and bamboo canes I marked out a processional way across the orchard,' he wrote to his sons on 7 December 1942, with the self-teasing note he often adopted to them, ironising his own grandiose schemes:

> I had in my mind an avenue of cherry trees as at Washington DC but I found, and was obliged to admit, that my avenue ran for about thirty yards through the Priepet Marshes [named after the Pripyat marshes, a vast area of wetland in Belarus and Ukraine]. I had sought to meet this difficulty by digging a deeper hole than was necessary and by filling in the bottom with rubble and clinkers. But there stood my cherry tree in a puddle – and I had to move it elsewhere, which destroys my avenue, my symmetry and my attempts at land drainage.

Still, in the spring the Orchard glows with new life. Armies of many different varieties of narcissus and the blossom of its many young fruit trees can be seen half a mile away across the fields, like a vision of renewal. The grass is allowed to grow deep into the summer so that the fritillaries that hang their heads among the hay can set seed. In the 1980s there were no more than a few dozen. Now there are hundreds, both the darkly glamorous snake's head fritillary, beloved by Vita, and their white cousins.

More than any other part of Sissinghurst, the Orchard has suffered in the last 40 years. Its ancient fruit trees laden with roses have in large part collapsed, and it has, for the time being, lost something of its otherworldly magic. The Great Storm in 1987 lashed it, and trees are slowly being replaced. Perhaps by 2039 something of the atmosphere of 1939 will have returned.

Opposite top *The Orchard in April, viewed from across the moat, itself edged with a mass of marsh marigolds* (Caltha palustris)

Two memorials

The Orchard is enhanced by two buildings which were the inspiration of Nigel Nicolson. The first, the Gazebo (opposite), a room which – as its name suggests – gazes at the view, was built in 1969 on the corner of the moat overlooking the Low Weald, as a memorial to his father Harold. The second, the boathouse, was built in 2002, looking down the northern arm of the moat. Along with the fenced ring of oak trees in the field beyond the moat, it stands as another memorial to him.

The Tower Lawn

The Tower Lawn fills the upper half of what was once Sissinghurst's great Elizabethan courtyard. A reproduction of an 18th-century engraving under the tower shows what it would have looked like in its prime. It is now at the crossing-point of Harold Nicolson's two controlling axes in the garden.

On the east side of the lawn, the severe dark line of the Yew Walk, planted in 1932, is the most radical modernist design statement at Sissinghurst. It destroys at a single stroke any idea that the garden was shaped by nothing but a nostalgic longing for the past.

Although magnolias were planted by Vita and Harold in the beds on the south side of the lawn in 1934, much of the planting along the beautiful pink west wall on both sides of the tower died in the severe winter of 1962–3. Although people tend to rush through this courtyard, as if it were a corridor, there are many beautiful things here: the climbing roses 'Albertine' and 'Paul's Lemon Pillar', as well as the clematises and the many exotics in the north-west corner. All post-date Vita's direct influence in the garden.

The damp, shady, sunken garden in the south-west corner, with a lion mask on the wall, began life as the Lion Pond, but it would not hold water, and in 1939 this was where Vita's thoughts first turned to a new kind of garden:

Vita to Harold, 12 December 1939
The Lion Pond is being drained. I have got what I hope will be a really lovely scheme for it: all white flowers with some clumps of very pale pink. White clematis, white lavender, white agapanthus, white double primroses, white anemones, white camellias, including giganteum in one corner and the pale peach-coloured *Primula pulverulenta*.

When Vita and Harold created the White Garden itself in the 1950s, the pale planting in this corner was changed to damp-loving ferns and irises.

Right The Lower Courtyard, with its neat box-edged beds Opposite A clematis montana, underplanted with Iris pseudacorus 'Variegata' and ferns, clothes the wall between the Tower Lawn and the Rose Garden

Cutting the hedges
Hedge-cutting takes place between May and November. 'Cutting all the hedges in the entire garden takes just over 1,000 hours,' the gardener Peter Fifield says. 'We use battery-powered hedge-cutters. This means no generator, no cables, less noise and no pollution. The hedges have been cut so precisely for so long that it is relatively easy to cut off the new, softer growth and 'feel' the face of the hedge with your cutters – as long as you keep your blades flat against the plane of the hedge!'

The Tower

Under the tower is the plaque by Reynolds Stone, which records, unfairly to Harold, Vita's making of the garden. Her workroom was on the first floor above. It was here, with her windows open on a warm summer day, that she could smell Sissinghurst around her, a 'softness about the air, a scent of musk and hay, a scent borne from the great white lilies and the tumbling roses'. This was, in its essence, Vita's tower, although others used it. From 1936 to 1939 Gwen St Aubyn, Harold's sister and Vita's lover, lived in the beautiful room on the upper-most floor and in the summer of 1940, as Vita wrote to Harold in London: 'The only nice thing that comes out of the war is that we now have a guard on top of the tower. In a steel helmet and rifle he looks most picturesque over the parapet.'

One or two privileged guests were allowed entry to her room itself. The writer and aesthete James Lees-Milne, who later became Harold's biographer, remembered a bewitching, dusky evening talking to her there:

The Gladstone bag

Vita kept all her notes and manuscripts in the turret beyond her workroom. Here in 1962, her son Nigel found the locked Gladstone bag which contained the manuscript confession of her love for Violet Trefusis. After Trefusis's own death ten years later, Nicolson published the manuscript as the basis for *Portrait of a Marriage*, his study of his parents' lives and sexuality.

There were no reservations of any kind. No topics were barred. Her curiosity about and understanding of human nature in all its aspects were limitless. Her sympathy with every human frailty and predicament was all embracing. This was the Vita I knew and most dearly loved. As dusk faded into night I watched the outline of her noble head against the chequered Tudor casements of the tower, would watch the tip of her cigarette from a long holder glow fiery red as she drew upon it, with constant but imperceptible inhalations so that her profile – always her profile of drooping eyelid, straight nose and soft rounded chin – would emerge from the darkness as in a momentary vision. I would smell, when I could no longer see, the cloud of Cypriot tobacco peculiarly her own; and listen to that deep slightly quavering, gently swelling voice, broken by eddies of short sharp laughter. 'Oh do tell me what happened next.' Then I understood what this unique woman's love meant to Harold.

From the Tower Lawn a small gateway in the north wall leads to the White Garden. It is called the Bishop's Gate, after the marble plaque let into the wall here, one of the treasures brought back by the Nicolsons from their first garden in Constantinople.

Left The Writing Room in the Tower, looking towards the sofa where Vita read her books Opposite Vita at her desk in 1948, photographed by John Gay Overleaf Vita's desk, framed by photographs of Harold and her dear friend and one-time lover, Virginia Woolf

The White Garden

Created in 1949–50, the White Garden was the last of the gardens at Sissinghurst to receive its identity. It became the culmination of Harold and Vita's joint vision of Sissinghurst. It fuses poetic theatricality, horticultural expertise and classical control. Nowhere in the garden is there a deeper sense of arrival.

The weeping pear and the lead cast of the Virgin, from the walnut original by Rosandić now in the Library, were both moved from the Rose Garden. Harold found some white gladioli, white irises, white pompom dahlias and the white Japanese anemones they both loved. Giant Arabian thistles, *Onopordum acanthium*, 'pure silver, eight feet high', would glamorise the beds and roses were trained up an avenue of almond trees.

By the late 1960s, many of the almond trees were dying so the gardening team decided to replace the avenue with a central rose arbour. 'The idea of something still supporting roses carried on,' explains Sissinghurst's researcher Monique Wolak, 'although the effect was of course different from an avenue of rose-covered trees.' The arbour was designed by Nigel Nicolson. He used paperclips to make his model, and their arched ends can still be detected.

North of the White Garden is a little garden, known as the Little North Garden. 'The garden was closed, but we knew it was an area that Vita and Harold gardened,' Head Gardener Troy Smith says. 'Using old photographs, the team reinstated the steps that were there and laid simple herringbone brick paths to connect to the surrounding buildings.' The planting – shades of white, blue and pale yellow – is loose and simple and blends well with the nearby Orchard. '*Robinia pseudoacacia* creates a white canopy you can see from the White Garden,' says Troy. 'As the garden is north facing we've added plants that can cope with some shade, such as anemones, gentians, nepeta, lilies, *Lucilia nivea* and *Iris sibirica*.'

Also on the north side of the garden, attached to the Priest's House, which had been the little Elizabethan garden banqueting house and was the Nicolsons' dining room and kitchen, is their shady summer dining table. It is in a little trellis-covered colonnade, called the Erechtheum after the temple on the Acropolis in Athens. It is made out of salvaged fragments of the Elizabethan house and, although a white wisteria grows there now, it was for many years covered in a vine which had been planted in 1935. Vita wrote about it in her wartime poem, *The Garden*:

> Green vine shade sweet airs breath; leaves lift;
> Tendrils in tenderest of shadows drift.
> Dog on the dappled ground your dappled
>   body lay.
> Black sun, black bumble bees, black grapes;
> Slim carven columns wreathed in vine;
> My little world of gently stirring shapes;
> Summer, the corn's last standing day.

Vita spent her last days in the bedroom above in June 1962, looking out through one window over the pale greys, creams, light pinks and greens of the White Garden, through the other over the woods and fields of Kent.

Right White tulips and wallflowers in spring
Opposite The White Garden is a frothy cloud of whites, greys and silvers – a delicious wedding cake of a garden. Note the grey willow-leaved Pyrus salicifolia *on the left*

A twilight garden

Vita had long been entranced by white flowers in the moonlight and in January 1950, before this garden existed, she had imagined it as it would be seen from the rough oak and box seat in the south-east corner of the garden:

> When you sit on this seat you will be turning your backs to the yew hedge and from there I hope you will survey a low sea of grey clumps of foliage, pierced here and there with tall white flowers. I cannot help hoping that the grey ghostly barn owl will sweep silently across a pale garden, next summer, in the twilight, the pale garden that I am now planting under the first flakes of snow.

Delos

'This is the last piece of the jigsaw in our plan to restore Vita and Harold's Sissinghurst into a softer, more romantic place,' Troy reflects. He and his team are currently working on an exciting transformation of the area known as Delos. 'At the moment it's just a canopy of magnolia trees with an underplanting of spring bulbs. It's very different now than it was in Harold and Vita's time. The new planting will have a Mediterranean feel and mimic the rocky landscape and building fragments found on the Greek island of Delos, the couple's inspiration for this area of the garden.' The planting with be loose with lots of self-seeders and feel a bit like an olive grove. Cork oaks and evergreen shrubs will be enlived in spring and summer with fleeting annuals such as nigellas, *Anemone coronaria*, tulips, irises.

'I'm honoured to bring to life their plans for Delos, an area of the garden which, over the years, has lost its original intent.'

Dan Pearson, garden designer

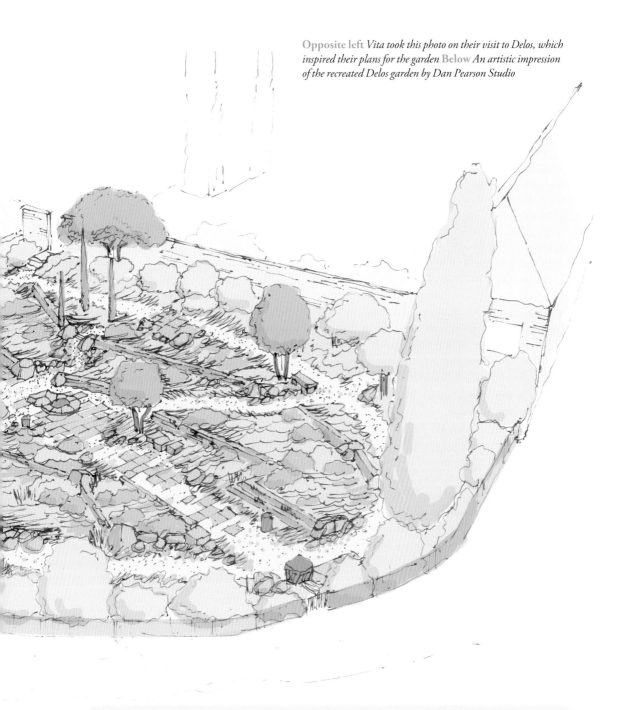

Dedicated to beauty

The modern Delos is yet another demonstration that Sissinghurst has not entered a sclerotic, rigidified old age, but continues to revivify its astonishingly strong traditions: horticultural excellence, the marriage of precision and naturalism, and an appetite for the overwhelmingly bold seasonal and chromatic effect – all this is put in the service of the idea that governs Sissinghurst as a whole: this is a place uncompromisingly dedicated to beauty.

The History of Sissinghurst as a Place

Beginnings

Sissinghurst is embedded in its woods. In every direction, looking out from the rooftop parapets of the Elizabethan tower, you see the woods of the Kentish Weald, the oaks above the chestnut and hazel understorey, the streams cutting shallow valleys in the underlying clay. The dragonflies dance in the wet hollows, and on summer nights you can hear the nightingales half a mile away across the fields.

About 50 miles south of London and 20 or so from the coast of the English Channel, the Sissinghurst landscape draws little from either. There is no sense of the sea, nor any of the urban. The woodland insulates this place from the outside world. Until the invention of tarmac in the 19th century, the roads of the Kentish Weald (the word is the same as 'Wald'; a forest) were virtually impassable for all but the hard dry months of high summer and early autumn.

It was as woodland pasture that the story of Sissinghurst begins. Some Stone Age tools have been found just south of the garden: a stone knife and a couple of scrapers. People were making their way here for the ironstone 3,000 years ago, and a beautiful gold ring, two strands twisted together, was found at the neighbouring farm of Bettenham, the jewellery of a minor Celtic chieftain picking his way through the great forest.

The Romans drove a road through here. Faint traces of it can be found in the shaped stones of a ford where its line crosses a small stream four miles south of Sissinghurst. But the Roman impact on Sissinghurst was small. A visitor found a tiny piece of Roman glass in the 1990s, lying on the grass just north of the Elizabethan barn, and a Roman coin was found by one of the gardeners digging over a bed of wallflowers outside the South Cottage. But that is all.

The story of settlement begins after the Romans left in the 5th century AD, when the invaders from northern Europe, sailing across the North Sea, came into north Kent, and started to make their inroads into the forest. The Sissinghurst woods were ideal for the Anglo-Saxon swineherds. Look at a map of Kent today and in the pattern of lanes which track across the county from the north you can still follow the naturally branching lines taken by these early, seasonally shifting farmers towards the nutritious autumn pastures. Until the 18th century, Sissinghurst was still officially part of a manor belonging to the Archbishops of Canterbury at the western edge of that city, a memory that the Weald was once an outer settlement – not the heart of southern England, but its colonial frontier.

Different ethnic groups settled different parts of the wood, some of them clearing the trees, in the way of all early colonists. Within two miles of Sissinghurst, there is a small settlement called Angley (the Angles' clearing). Pigs fattened here in the way they couldn't in the rest of the county. The drove roads by which they were driven into the Weald still exist, coming over the Downs at Charing, past Smarden and approaching Sissinghurst on the old track across the fields from the north called Blackberry Lane. As for Sissinghurst itself, the earliest recorded form of the name, in a medieval charter, is 'Saxingherste', probably meaning 'the wood occupied by the Saxons.'

Opposite *Mist rising from the Orchard*

Sissinghurst began life as a Saxon pig farm, feeding off the acorns which the all-present oaks still scatter in profusion every autumn. Gradually, people began to live all year round in the Wealden wood. The autumn pastures became the focus of permanent settlements. Sissinghurst became a small moated manor house, lived in by a family who shared their name with the place, the de Saxingherstes. They fought as knights for the Kings of England in their French wars, the younger sons went into the church, and their house was important enough for Edward I, the great warrior king, to stay here with his retinue in 1279, 1299 and 1305. It may be that this part of the kingdom had nowhere much better to choose. It was never rich. The King needed guides to show him the way through the Weald. No great landlords dominated the mixture of woodland and pasture. Small farmers raised their sheep and wove the wool into cloth.

Nothing except the moat survives of that medieval house, nor any record of it, but just across the fields at Bettenham, a small farmhouse, which still retains the name Bettenham Manor, has its own moat and its cluster of medieval fishponds. There, on a cool evening, as the mist comes up from the damp low-lying meadows in which it sits, and with the roach and rudd rising in the ponds, something of the atmosphere of the medieval Sissinghurst can still be recovered.

In the 13th century the de Saxingherstes were succeeded, perhaps through marriage, by the de Berhams. Intriguingly, this outer corner of the parish of Cranbrook was of the highest status. Although they had lands elsewhere in Kent, they lived here and married the daughters of rich Cranbrook cloth makers. They were magistrates, commanding the local militia, and one acted as Sheriff of Kent. The de Berhams and their neighbours the de Bettenhams were the two families which contributed most to the early 15th-century rebuilding of Cranbrook church.

The Bakers

That medieval Sissinghurst, a place of deep-rooted stability, was utterly transformed in the 16th century, as money, political ambition, an acquisitive toughness and a reaching for glamour and gloriousness all, quite suddenly, landed on the site of the ancient manor. This arrival of the modern was in the hands of a dynamic Cranbrook family, the Bakers, who had been established there for at least a century. They had married into the prestigious de Bettenham family in the 1300s and by the end of the 15th century, perhaps by connection with the cloth trade, and by dealing in a buoyant land market, had begun to gather property and wealth.

The de Berhams sold part of the Sissinghurst estate to Thomas Baker of Cranbrook in about 1490. Not until 1533 did the Bakers acquire the site of the house. The buyer was Thomas Baker's grandson, Sir John, a tough-minded and ambitious lawyer and politician, who weaved his way through the maze of royal service in the reigns of Henry VIII, Edward VI and Queen Mary. He became in succession Attorney General, Chancellor of the Exchequer and Speaker of the House of Commons. He was a fierce and lifelong Catholic and during the reign of Queen Mary he was known, at least to Protestants, as 'Butcher Baker' (later improved to 'Bloody Baker') for his judicial

harrying of people he saw as heretics. Like all royal servants in early modern England, he adapted to survive, moving this way and that to accommodate the changing religious persuasions of his masters and making sure that his service to the crown resulted in his own enrichment. As land from the Dissolution of the Monasteries came on to the market, Baker, at the centre of the royal administrative machinery, was in prime position to acquire it. By the time he died in 1558, Sir John Baker had amassed an enormous fortune and an estate of many thousands of acres scattered across Kent and Sussex, raising himself up to the first rank of the gentry.

He remained loyal to Kent, instructing his executors to bury him in Cranbrook church 'if I die within three score myles therof.' No documents survive to describe the building history of Sissinghurst, but it seems likely that in the 1530s Sir John Baker built the entrance arch and its flanking gables, and maybe the rest of the long front range. Its Gothic windows and its overall severity and simplicity reflect the sobriety and seriousness of the man, but the house to which it gave entrance (which, it is now thought, may have been the de Berhams' manor house) was certainly substantial enough to entertain the French ambassador in 1551 and Queen Mary in 1557.

Sᵗ John Baker, Speaker 1547.
From an Original picture in the possession of
William Baker Esqᵗ. of Norwich.

Sir Richard Baker

Sir John's son, Sir Richard Baker, was very different and he undoubtedly revolutionised the sober manor house his father had built or acquired. The father knew what was coming, admonishing his son directly in his will, even as he left him his fortune:

> To myne oldest sonne Richard Bakere goddes blessinge and myne and all such my plate of siluer and gilt &e. and all other stuffe and utensils of houshold in my manor mesuage and house of Cessyngherst. And I charge the my sonne Richarde that above all things thowe serve God and thy soueraigne lord and lady the Kinge and queen [Philip and Mary] applye thy lernynge, be curtesse and gentill to euery bodie... avoyde Brybery, extortion, corruption and dissimulacon, eschewe Idlenes, applie the to vertuose exercise, be faythfull and true in worde and deede and holly put thy truste in Almightie God wt humble callinge to hym for grace with laudes and thanks for all they benefites...

This very sage advice from one generation to another was ignored. Richard abandoned his political career and within a year or two of receiving his huge inheritance he began spending it on transforming Sissinghurst into the most magnificent display house of the Kentish Weald.

He converted the 700 acres surrounding the house into a glorious but unproductive deer park (of which there is no mention in his father's lifetime), surrounded by an expensive oak pale seven miles long. He built the great tower both as a viewing platform for the hunt and as a monumental gateway to the enormous Renaissance courtyard house that lay beyond: a columned portico, stone balls on the gable tops, pilasters and strapwork on the surface of the brick, a wainscoted and vaulted gallery 120 feet long, elegantly carved and painted, decorated throughout with the huge windows that the Elizabethans loved, 'every room so spacious, so well lighted and so high roofed within'. Thirty-eight hearths, many of them in marble chimneypieces, burned in the buildings.

The building now known as the Priest's House, although extended in the 17th century, began as a large-windowed pavilion on the edge of the garden looking out across the landscape, a place in which elegant indoor picnics could be held. One arm of the old moat was partly filled in and lined with a beautiful brick wall to make a bowling green, or at least an outdoor gallery in which to stroll in the sunshine.

The way this great Elizabethan house sat within its landscape was a precise reflection of late 16th-century Renaissance ideals. Philip Sidney's description of Basilius's house in Arcadia might have been a description of Sissinghurst as it was in its days of completeness and glory:

> Truly a place for pleasantness, for it being set upon such an insensible rising of the ground as you are come to a pretty height before almost you perceive that you ascend, it gives the eye lordship over a good large circuit, which according to the nature of the country, being diversified between hills and dales, woods and plain, one place more clear, another more darksome, it seems a pleasant picture of nature, with lovely lightsomeness and artificial shadows.

Opposite top The Tower and Lower Courtyard
Opposite bottom Engraving of Sissinghurst Castle, view south-east from the Tower, *by Richard Godfrey, c.1750*

A royal visitor

The Queen herself was persuaded to visit for three days in August 1573. Richard Baker, to be knighted a few days later, presented her with a silver-gilt cup on whose crystal lid a lion held forth the royal coat of arms. There was hunting in the park and revels by night. The house was the hero, 'by day time, on every side so glittering by glass; by nights, by continual brightness of candle, fire, and torch-light, transparent through the lightsome windows...'

Sissinghurst, in the County of Kent.

Decline

Sissinghurst's moment of greatness had been brief. In the 17th century, it entered its long decline. Perhaps the Bakers had overreached themselves. Perhaps the stern, ruthless drive of the mid-16th-century Sir Thomas Baker had dissipated itself in the Romantic dreams of chivalry and the hunt, to which rich young Elizabethan men, like his son Sir Richard, were chronically prey. For whatever reason, the coherence began to collapse. The local puritan population – one of the densest and fiercest clusters of Puritanism in England was in Cranbrook – attacked both the deer park and the Bakers' ironworks. The Bakers moved to London. They had always had property in Southwark. They now acquired a house, richly furnished, in Covent Garden. Lists of those taking communion in the early 17th century show them to be absent from Sissinghurst and the place occupied only by their servants.

The Bakers, in a move that was highly suspicious for the puritan mind, had their own chapel consecrated at Sissinghurst in 1639, a hint perhaps that they had remained secret Catholic sympathisers ever since the Reformation. The excuse given by Sir John Baker (Sir Richard's great-grandson) was that 'by reason of deep and fowle ways (especially in winter) he and his family are not able without much trouble and danger duly to frequent the parish church in Cranbrook'. He installed his own chaplain, who may have lived in the little garden pavilion since known (perhaps sardonically?) as the Priest's House. It was certainly extended at the time. All this may add up to some evidence that the Bakers, in the changed atmosphere of the 1630s, could at last in secret return to the High Church practice of their forefathers. Certainly, the chapel was richly furnished with 'a fayre silver bason, a silver pott for the wine and a silver challice with a cover for the communion and a silver plate with a bason for the font, all double guilt.'

Golden accoutrements of this kind were not to be found in the Cranbrook church. The words preached at the dedication of the new chapel have survived. Robert Abbot, vicar of Cranbrook, in a gruesomely obsequious sermon dedicated to 'His Honourable Friend, The right Worshipfull Sir John Baker Baronet', describes the new chapel:

> built and furnished with cost: Profit therefore is engaged and hath given way to the devout worship of God here. It is built by a garden of pleasure, a parlour of plenty… Joseph's tomb was in a garden, to be a monitor (in the midst of refreshments) to the way of immortalitie.

This is the only record that Renaissance Sissinghurst also had its pleasure garden. Maybe it was here that the bushes of Rose des Maures, the rose discovered at Sissinghurst by Vita in 1930 (and for a while called *Rosa gallica* 'Sissinghurst Castle') were growing?

During the Civil War, the Bakers, as one would expect, sided with the King against Parliament and were punished for doing so. At a time when a perfectly good manor house could be built for £150, fines of at least £8,000 were exacted and goods sequestered. The rich furniture from the house in Covent Garden was seized and sold. Sir John wriggled, telling Parliament 'he much disliked the King's proceedings', but it was no good. Documents from the late 1640s detailing the sale of his estates all across the south of England are to be found in the county records, a dismal account of the end of any pretensions to greatness.

Opposite A view through the entrance arch, bathed in warm summer light

Collapse

Sir John died in 1653 and was succeeded by his son, another Sir John. In an act of what looks at this distance like pure bravado, performed at a time when parks all over England had been invaded by the people and their deer killed and stolen, he restored the park pale in 1657 around its full seven-mile length. But he was dead within four years, and his widow lingered on in the impoverished house. This was the beginning of the collapse. There was no male heir to the Baker line, and the property descended to four daughters, all of whom eventually married away. In the 1690s, individual rooms in the house were let out as apartments for people taking a cure at 'the old admired well' in the park. The well has disappeared, but it was probably in the boggy ground somewhere near where the present lane leaves the main road. Otherwise, Sissinghurst lay empty for years, a rotting hulk, inhabited by lawless servants. Senseless murders were committed here. Horace Walpole passed by in 1749 and found it 'a park in ruins and a house in ten times greater ruins.'

When the family, looking to recover the £9,000 mortgage on the estate, rented it to the government as a prison for up to 3,000 captured French seamen during the Seven Years War (1756–63), the place was as good as destroyed. It became as brutal and horrible as any 18th-century gaol. Frenchmen held elsewhere in England were threatened with being sent to Sissinghurst if they misbehaved. In the Public Record Office in Kew, a thick file of letters from the French prisoners at Sissinghurst has survived, detailing the brutalities to which they were subjected: torture, bullying, bribery, extortion. One guard was killed when a bucket was dropped on his head from the top of the Tower. A prisoner was shot dead for not extinguishing the light in his room. When the circumstances were investigated, it turned out that he had never had a light lit at all: the guard had mistaken a reflection on one of the diamond panes of the windows. The barn became a hospital. The upper reaches of what is now the car-park were the prison cemetery.

With barricades around the buildings and braziers on high poles to illuminate the perimeter at night, this is the period at which Sissinghurst first became known as Sissinghurst Castle, the name not of a medieval fortress but of a modern, state-run, armed prisoner-of-war camp. The name may first have been used with a hint of irony.

After the war was over, an account was made of the dilapidations to the house. The entire property was valued at precisely £300. The inventory of damage records the destruction of a great house:

To 2,092 foot of glass destroyed and great damage to the winder frames by many iron bars being gon £100

To the Long Gallery by destroying neer two hundred yards of wainscott with a rich entablature carved, marble chimney piece broke down and woodwork greatly damaged. £50

To great damage done in the best garden by the wall, fruit and other trees all destroyed and not even the rump of a shrub or tree left. £20

When late 18th-century travellers happened to pass by the pitiable ruins, the word they most often used was 'dismal'. The great Elizabethan courtyard was quarried for roadstone. The parish poorhouse was set up in the stables. Cows grazed the courtyards and sheltered from the rain in the turrets of the Bakers' tower. In 1855, the mid-Victorian landowners, the Mann-Cornwallises of Linton, built a handsome new brick farmhouse just beyond the Castle buildings and took the estate in hand, regularising field boundaries, draining the wettest of the fields, planting new hop gardens and selling the hops to the London brewers: the railway had arrived, and the nearest station was a mere five miles away. The old house lay in the background, providing cottages for a couple of farm labourers and a dumping ground for any passing rubbish.

Above *A naive painting of Sissinghurst Castle showing it being used as a prisoner-of-war camp, showing the killing of several French prisoners, 1761* Left *Engraving of Sissinghurst Castle, 1760*

Rescue

When Sissinghurst was put up for sale in 1928, no one wanted it. It lay on the market for two years unsold. Only in the wet spring of 1930 did Vita Sackville-West and Harold Nicolson hear of the place from the poet Dorothy Wellesley, who had been her lover. If she had been a boy, Vita, the only daughter of Lord Sackville, would have inherited the great Sackville house of Knole near Sevenoaks. She was denied that inheritance because of her sex and was instead living in Long Barn, a small medieval house not far from Sevenoaks. When a new battery chicken farm threatened their house, she and Harold were forced to leave. The sales particulars for Sissinghurst described the splendid Victorian Castle farmhouse – ten bedrooms, 'well matured grounds with lawn and rhododendrons' – the 500 acres of wood and land and, almost as an afterthought, some 'picturesque old buildings' in the grounds.

Above This aerial view of the tower and surviving buildings was taken in 1932, just two years after Sissinghurst had been acquired by Vita and Harold

It was of course the ruins to which Vita and Harold were drawn: gaunt, partly unroofed, damp and bleak. They wavered. Harold, on 13 April, after a second look, considered it 'big broken down, and sodden', but Vita had the money, and it was her choice. They bought it for £12,375. There was no electricity, no running water, no drains, no heating and scarcely a fireplace that worked. But this was the invitation: to pour their energies into redemption of the past.

Harold collected foxgloves from the wood in an old pram. They would have preferred to make the paths of York stone as they now are. But there wasn't enough money, so paving-stone-sized slabs of rough concrete were cast on site. What statues they bought were cheap. Only what they inherited from Vita's mother after her death in 1936 – the bronze and lead urns, the statue of the Bacchante now in the Spring Garden, the bench at the head of the moat walk designed by Lutyens – were of undeniable quality. The beautiful stoneware pot in the centre of the White Garden, a 17th-century Chinese oil or ginger jar, had been bought by Harold in Cairo for £10.

The bones of the garden were made extraordinarily quickly: by 1932 what is now the White Garden, the Tower Lawn, the Spring Garden, the Cottage Garden, the Yew Walk and the Nuttery had all been laid out. The hedges and trees which would in time give the garden its form were already largely planted. By the end of that decade, the new walls closing off the Rose Garden and the north side of the Upper Courtyard had been built and the orchard designed.

Something of the atmosphere in the early Sissinghurst emerges in a letter from Vita to Harold describing a day in April 1936:

How people can say life is dull in the country beats me. Take the last 24 hours here. An extremely drunken man had left his pony to be tried in the mowing machine. So it was put in the mowing machine; I watched; all seemed satisfactory; I went away. So did the mowing machine. Kennelly [the gardener] sent it away without saying a word to me or to Copper [the chauffeur/handyman] who is responsible for it. Copper arrived in my room and abused Kennelly. I went and cursed Kennelly, who indeed was in the wrong. In the evening at about 9, I was told that Punnett [the builder] wanted to see me. I went out. He was in tears, having just found his old father drowned in the engine tank, and a note written to himself saying it was suicide.

Next morning, ie today, George [the man-servant] came to fetch me: Copper would like to speak to me. I found Copper in the garden room covered in blood with a great gash in his head. Kennelly had come into the garage and knocked him down without any warning. He had fallen unconscious, and had come round to find Kennelly throwing buckets of water over him. He had then tried to strangle Kennelly, and they had only been separated by the arrival of Mrs Copper. So I sent Copper to the doctor in George's car, and meanwhile sent for the police. Accompanied by the policeman I went out in search of Kennelly, whom we found very frightened and white. He was ordered to go and pack his things and leave at once. So that was that and we are now without a gardener.

Right *Vita at work in the garden in the Rose Garden, 1930*

After the war

The war interrupted progress, and for six years Sissinghurst roughened and thickened. Hay crops were taken off the lawns. Weeds invaded the beds. Jack Vass, the head gardener and mainstay of Sissinghurst from 1939 onwards, volunteered for the RAF in 1941, saying to Vita as he left: 'Look after the hedges. We can get the rest back later.' Dutifully, if a little amateurishly, Harold and Vita clipped the yews and pleached the limes until he returned. Vita knew she couldn't make Sissinghurst without him. One year he planted 12,000 Dutch bulbs, and in 1946 she prayed to her diary:

> Oh dear kind God, please let Vass live strong and healthy until he is eighty at least, and never let him be tempted away to anyone else's garden. His keenness is so endless, and nothing is too much trouble. Besides he's so good looking, so decorative.

Vass finally left in 1957, after he and Vita had argued over something to do with the Sissinghurst Flower Show. He was succeeded by other stopgap gardeners but Sissinghurst entered a new phase with the arrival in October 1959 of Pam Schwerdt and Sibylle Kreutzberger. They remained joint head gardeners until 1990 and in their refinement and heightening over three decades of the ideas which Vita and Harold had begun here, they should be seen as joint creators of the garden.

'We have done our best and made a garden where none was.'

Vita Sackville-West, in a letter to Harold Nicolson, written shortly before her death

The Sissinghurst they found on their arrival was rough and untended. The fig trees in the Rose Garden were occupying three-quarters of the flower beds, with no room for flowers. Sibylle Kreutzberger remembers Vita and Harold setting off for a winter cruise in late 1959 and leaving the two new gardeners to tackle the pruning:

> We hacked away for weeks while she was away. There used to be a winter secretary who came in and sent Vita's post off to wherever they'd gone to. One day this secretary came round the corner and the whole Rose Garden was strewn with branches the thickness of your thigh. 'I do hope Lady Nicolson hasn't got second sight,' she said.

Sissinghurst had never been a comfortable place. In the winter it was cold, and there was no spare room for guests to stay the night. The electric heating system in the Library had unaccountably been installed in the ceiling, creating the conditions for a deliciously warm attic, but a persistently frozen room beneath. Even so, Harold and Vita did not live in poverty. They had two gardeners, a chauffeur, a cook, a lady's maid, two secretaries and other servants. Grapes, peaches, apples, pears, raspberries, gooseberries, cucumbers, tomatoes, mangetouts, cabbage, aubergines, squashes, pumpkins and quinces were all grown for their table.

As Harold had predicted, Vita's entire inherited fortune poured into the creation and maintenance of Sissinghurst. Even when ill, she continued until 1961 writing her articles for the *Observer* because she needed the income.

When Vita died in June 1962, she knew that she had created something of lasting value. 'We have done our best,' she wrote to Harold in November 1961, 'and made a garden where none was.' He survived her by six years, sad and lonely. Visitors would see him sitting in the garden with the tears running down his cheeks.

Opposite Vita and Harold on the Tower steps in 1960

The National Trust

Vita left Sissinghurst to her younger son Nigel Nicolson. He was faced with large death duties to pay on her estate. His only options were to sell everything; sell the farm and keep the house and garden; or persuade the Treasury that in lieu of death duties they would accept the entire property and give it to the National Trust. Nicolson was particularly concerned that his parents' greatest creation should neither be erased under new ownership; nor that the bond between garden and landscape at Sissinghurst should be broken by selling off the surrounding land. The National Trust was the only option that could ensure these connections remained whole. But it was also one that Vita had dreaded. Nigel had dared broach the subject of the National Trust with her a few years earlier. 'I said Never never never,' she wrote that evening:

Au grand jamais jamais jamais. Never, never, never… Nigel can do what he likes when I am dead, but so long as I live no Nat Trust or any other foreign body shall have my darling. No, no. Over my corpse or my ashes. Not otherwise. It is bad enough to have lost my Knole, but they shan't take S/hurst from me. That, at least, is my own.

The Trust, on its part, was sceptical. How could an organism as transitory as a garden, and one so dependent on the taste and vision of its original makers, be preserved in perpetuity? Not until 1967 did Nigel Nicolson persuade the Trust that Sissinghurst was a viable entity and in March that year it entered the Trust's ownership.

Alongside his care for his parents' garden, he embarked on a 20-year campaign to honour their memory. In a steady stream, he published their diaries, letters and autobiographical fragments. He commissioned books describing the making of the garden and biographies of both his mother and father. Above all, he published in 1972 *Portrait of a Marriage*, an account and an explanation of how both Harold and Vita, although both homosexual and both serially unfaithful to the other, survived the traumatic early years of their marriage to shape together, largely at Sissinghurst, a life of extraordinarily profound love and respect.

The widespread international success of these books stimulated an ever-growing stream of visitors to the garden. In 1966, there were 28,000 visitors. Two years later that had doubled. Today's steady stream of visitors has meant that Sissinghurst is better funded now than it has been since the 16th century, and the flow of funds has meant that buildings have been repointed and repaired, concrete paths replaced and equipment renewed. Sissinghurst, season after season, now glows with its own wellbeing.

Below left The Gazebo and dove house in the Orchard in spring
Below Vita and Harold's son, Nigel, who persuaded the National Trust to look after Sissinghurst in 1967

Sissinghurst today

Troy Smith, head gardener at Sissinghurst since 2013, has been connected to the garden for many years: 'I had my first encounter with the soil at Sissinghurst over 20 years ago when I worked here as a gardener, a period that set the tone for rest of my gardening career. I learned to love detail. I learned great techniques and I learned to be inquisitive about plants and critical in their effective juxtaposition. Along with the immense privilege of gardening within this garden, I was also immediately aware of the responsibility and huge challenge that goes with it.'

The task for the gardeners is the subtlest possible one. 'We must truly understand what we've got and reassess what we do,' says Troy, 'shifting from a focus around standards and presentation to things that really matter: not least gardening in a way that seeks to recapture the distinctive qualities of Vita and Harold's Sissinghurst: a more reflective, romantic, slower, deeper place than much of what the modern Sissinghurst has become. True to the garden's historic distinctiveness, fully informed of the history and significance, we will take what is great and intensify the enjoyment.'

Harold and Vita never thought of Sissinghurst as complete and finished. 'How I wish I had another 50 years to look forward to,' Vita wrote towards the end of her life, 'and 10 gardeners and 10 thousand pounds – then we would restore the lakes and make a water garden down there and a lovely approach to it via the calf orchard with avenues of peaches and nectarines, very straight and simple with mown grass walks and bulbs for spring.'

Another world

The paradox of the preservation of Sissinghurst is that its beauty consists of a dialogue between the old and the new, between a sense of daring and adventure and a romance that looks back to a softer, purer time. It must constantly negotiate the line between what is and what might be. It is a dream made real; or reality dragged towards the condition of a dream. 'How fair the flowers unaware,' Vita had written when she was a young woman:

> That do not know what beauty is!
> Fair without knowing they are fair,
> With poets and gazelles they share
> Another world than this.

In many ways, Sissinghurst became that other world.

Opposite Troy Smith, Sissinghurst's talented head gardener **Right** *Wisteria venusta 'Alba Plena' on the pergola by the Priest's House*

The Estate

The garden at Sissinghurst sits within some 470 acres of mixed Wealden landscape. The southern half of the farm is clothed in about 200 acres of woodland. A belt of permanent pasture surrounds the house and garden. The northern and eastern fields are currently used for arable crops. Although this landscape nurtures birds of prey, nightingales and woodpeckers, as well as a dazzling display of summer dragonflies and damselflies, much of what can now be seen is of a relatively recent date.

There are some ancient outlines here. The main road from Cranbrook to Biddenden which runs along the ridge to the south of the wood; and the bridleway on the northern side of Sissinghurst, now called Blackberry Lane, are both the descendants of ancient trackways which led into the heart of the Weald from the more open country to the east and north. Both roads almost certainly pre-dated any settlement here.

From the Middle Ages, though, very little seems to have survived. Faint outlines of ridge-and-furrow in the wood and in the small orchard next to the main road – only visible in the snow or in evening light – are the remains of medieval cultivation. Otherwise, everything here was overwhelmed by Sir Richard Baker's creation of his deer park in the 1560s. One or two magnificent pollarded oaks from that park still survive, at least 400 years old, and the bank on which the park pale or fence was built can still be traced for much of its length. A set of fishponds may well have been made along the valley of the little stream that runs to the south of the garden.

This was the moment in which Sissinghurst was given its identity, of which the symbol and central fact remains the Tower. 'People always talk about the view of the farm from the garden,' says Lead Ranger Peter Dear. 'But what about the view of the castle from the farm? Wherever you are, you can always see the Tower.

You catch glimpses of it and it is a homely sight. It's a familiar face – it welcomes you. It is what makes Sissinghurst Sissinghurst. If you can see the Tower, you know where you are. I think it's one of the reasons people love this place as much as they do.'

After the decline of the Baker family, the Sissinghurst landscape was radically reshaped. The Elizabethan parkland was divided up into fields that were usable for a rich and productive mixed farm (always referred to in the 19th century as 'The Old Cow', because she could be milked so often and so fruitfully). A substantial Victorian farmhouse was built in 1855 by the landlords, the Mann-Cornwallises, whose initials still appear on the weather vanes above the Tower. At the end of the 19th century and on into the 20th, chestnuts were planted throughout the woods. Poles coppiced from them for fencing and the hop gardens proved a valuable cash crop.

Below *Aerial view of the tower* **Opposite** *Harvest time in the fields surrounding Sissinghurst*

The estate in the 20th century

One of the ironies of Sissinghurst is that as the great house was dismantled and its remains rotted, the farm around it thrived. When Vita and Harold came here in 1930, it was being farmed by Captain A.O.R. Beale, a hero in the First World War who had become one of Kent's most progressive farmers. It was a model of what a Wealden farm might be. Seven men worked under him, milking two dairy herds, one at Sissinghurst, one a mile away at Bettenham (which Vita would later also buy), keeping pigs, chickens, sheep and beef cattle, growing hops, peas, wheat, barley and oats, with three orchards, one of Worcester apples, one of Bramleys and the other of plums. They made hay and cider, they cut faggots from the wood, they carted enormous quantities of farmyard manure out on to the fields, and they delivered milk to the dairy in Cranbrook. Year after year, ploughing, rolling, harrowing, pruning, hedging, woodcutting, sowing, hop-stringing, sheep-dipping, mowing, haymaking, baling, cutting the clover, clearing the river weed, harvesting the cereals, picking the apples and then the hops, year after year, the seasons turned. And within the framework of that year and that landscape, Vita and Harold made their garden. This burgeoning wholeness of the surrounding landscape, a living and fertile version of the fullness Vita had celebrated in her long Virgilian poem *The Land*, was a spur to make the garden itself good again.

In the last half of the 20th century, as the garden at Sissinghurst entered its most glorious phase, the landscape around it declined. The demands and pressures of the agricultural market meant that the rich variety of Sissinghurst became deeply diminished. The dairy herds, the pigs, chickens, orchards and the hops all disappeared. Hedges were taken out and fields enlarged. By the end of the century, there were no employees on Sissinghurst Castle Farm, and the land was let to four different farmers who had their main businesses elsewhere.

Since then, however, the National Trust has begun to reverse the decline. New hedges have been planted and gates installed. Conservation margins have been established around the fields. The woods, which were severely damaged in the 1987 storm, are gradually coming back into order. The yellowhammers and sky-larks, which had virtually disappeared, are now back in numbers and breeding. Peter Dear, the lead ranger who lives here with his family, has wide-ranging plans for increasing the rough, thickety woodland which nightingales enjoy; for half-flooding parts of the stream valley to increase the all-too-valuable marshy habitats; and has already laid long stretches of hedge which had been neglected for decades. The connections between garden and landscape which were so central an aspect of Vita's vision of Sissinghurst – it is not a house with a garden; it is a house in a garden in a landscape – are once again coming alive.

Below *View of sheep grazing in late October* **Opposite** *Cattle market, with Sissinghurst Castle and the oast houses in the background, 1930s*

The Vegetable Garden and the Sissinghurst Farm Project

In 2008 the National Trust, as part of its countrywide food policy, decided to change the relationship between the heart of Sissinghurst and its surrounding farmland. Together with Adam Nicolson, it decided that it would be a good idea – for the landscape, for local food sourcing and for a sense of vitality at Sissinghurst – to try to grow the food for the restaurant on the farm. Today Sissinghurst Vegetable Garden supplies over six tonnes of fresh food to the Granary restaurant and Old Dairy café. The growing season continues all year round with the Vegetable Garden supplying a wonderful and varied selection of salads, brassicas, root crops, tender vegetables and soft fruits all grown under a 'no-dig' system. The Vegetable Garden also supplies the plant shop with a range of crops and young vegetable plants so visitors can take a taste of Sissinghurst home with them.

Today, Sissinghurst is a mixed farm managed by a tenant farmer who keeps beef cattle, sheep and pigs and produces a wide variety of arable crops. The Trust also looks after a productive orchard and a nut platt of Kentish cobs.

Opposite Watering salad crops in August in the Vegetable Garden; a rich crop of courgettes **Below** *Dahlias in the Cutting Garden; inside the glasshouse* **Overleaf** *Vita and Harold outside the South Cottage in 1960, just two years before her death*

The Cutting Garden and Nursery

Twice a week visitors can enjoy a peek behind the scenes of the garden and enjoy a visit to the cut flower garden. This working area is where the team grow flowers for cutting which are used in the restaurant, tower and the library. The gardeners also use this area to focus on growing trial plants for the garden as well as biennials, such as foxgloves and sweet William, planted out when they are ready to flower. They also grow a duplicate selection of all the irises in the garden and have developed an area dedicated to growing many different varieties of delphinium – a celebration of the fact that Vita was president of the Delphinium Society.

The Nursery plays a vital role in supporting the garden, each year around 20,000 annuals, perennials and herbs are propagated on site from seeds and cuttings collected directly from the garden by our senior propagator. The plants are tended and grown in the nurseries, glasshouses and cold frames with help from the gardeners and a team of volunteers. Once ready the plants are destined for a variety of uses including the beds and borders of the garden, the many pots and troughs situated around the property and as stock plants as part of the conservation of Sissinghurst's important plant collection. The Nursery also grows in the region of 15,000 plants for sale in our plant shop, offering visitors the unique opportunity to buy plants they can see growing in this historic garden.